1966 BENJAMIN F. FAIRLESS MEMORIAL LECTURES

Library of Congress Catalog Card Number 67-20667

Management: a humanist art

David E. Lilienthal

© 1967 CARNEGIE INSTITUTE OF TECHNOLOGY

Distributed by Columbia University Press

New York-London

The Benjamin F. Fairless Memorial Lectures endowment fund has been established at Carnegie Institute of Technology to support an annual series of lectures. An internationally known figure from the worlds of business, government, or education will be invited each year to present three lectures at Carnegie under the auspices of its Graduate School of Industrial Administration. In general, the lectures will be concerned with some aspects of business or public administration; the relationships between business and government, management and labor; or a subject related to the themes of preserving economic freedom, human liberty, and the strengthening of individual enterprise — all of which were matters of deep concern to Mr. Fairless throughout his career.

The lecturer will, whenever possible, spend three weeks in residence on the Carnegie Campus, during which time he will be available for discussions with faculty and students.

Mr. Fairless was president of United States Steel Corporation for fifteen years, and chairman of the board from 1952 until his retirement in 1955. A friend of Carnegie Institute of Technology for many years, he served on the board of trustees from 1952 until his death. In 1959 he was named honorary chairman of the board. He was also a leader and co-chairman of Carnegie Tech's ten-year development program, from its beginning in 1957.

1966

seven

David E. Lilienthal, a founder of TVA and former chairman of the Atomic Energy Commission, is now chairman and chief executive officer of Development and Resources Corporation, a private, world-wide firm providing services for development of natural resources in countries all over the world.

A founding director of the Tennessee Valley Authority, Mr. Lilienthal was its chairman from 1941 until 1946. He was chairman of the Atomic Energy Commission from 1946 until 1950, having earlier been chairman of the State Department's Board of Consultants on International Control of Atomic Energy. He is the author of *TVA: Democracy on the March; Big Business: A New Era; This I Do Believe; Change, Hope, and the Bomb;* and the three-volume *Journals of David E. Lilienthal.*

I. Management: a humanist art

I. Management: a humanist art

That the distinguished committee of friends of Benjamin Fairless and of this institution, sponsoring this lecture series, should invite me to join in paying tribute to the achievements and to the character of Benjamin Fairless is an honor, and one that I highly prize. And that Carnegie Tech, a leader in technical and industrial education, should also be an outstanding leader in the arts and the humanities, adds a dimension which I find peculiarly appropriate in honoring the memory of Benjamin Fairless, who was not only an outstanding industrial leader but also a warm and intelligent supporter of the arts and the humanities.

The motif of these three lectures, the subject I shall seek to explore with you can be simply stated: the ability to get things done.

This capability has flourished in the free and robust air of America as nowhere else on earth. And Benjamin Fairless was a great exemplar of this special and distinctive kind of American genius. Benjamin Fairless got things done through the instrumentality of a large private corporation, the United States Steel Corporation. As I wrote in a book* — published fifteen years ago — which shocked some of my friends at the time, but no longer does, and I think as most people now surely recognize, big business is or can be a vital and a beneficial social force.

But most of us also recognize that public enterprises and governmental activities play an essential role in the building of our country's life. It's true there are people who still look with suspicion and even with disdain on big private business. Even more people, I should judge, have difficulty believing that anything that is run by government can be well done.

I'd like to recite to you one example that occurred in the hills of East Tennessee. When we lived in the little town of Norris, Tennessee, my wife used to get her eggs from a small farmer. He'd appear at our door about twice a week with his basket of eggs on his arm. About this time, there was a very big

---

Big Business: A New Era. Harper, 1953

industrial activity being built nearby, at Oak Ridge. It was very secret, at that time, very hush-hush and mysterious. Now Oak Ridge is famous as the place where the first atomic material for weapons was produced. For several months Mr. Johnson didn't appear at our door and, of course, we all assumed that he was working at Oak Ridge. Then one day he reappeared with his basket of eggs on his arm. My wife said, "Mr. Johnson, we've missed you. Where have you been?" He said, "That's a secret." But, he said, "You've been a customer of mine for a long time and I'll tell you. I've been working at Oak Ridge. But I quit." My wife said, "But why did you quit?" "Well, I seen all that work going on over there; all those great big factory buildings, all those roads and things. The Government's spending an awful lot of money, and I just thought it all over and I decided that whatever it was that the Government was afixing to make over there, it'd be cheaper if they went out and bought it."

My purpose in these lectures is to describe my concept of the manager's function of leadership in the crisis areas of the world's life today and tomorrow.

I conceive of the managerial function as a humanist art, with the development of the latent capabilities of people as its basic goal and purpose. At the outset, however, I should recognize that there are many other concepts of the role of the manager and of the function of management.

Certainly the notion that management is a humanist art is a far cry from some of the narrower meanings of the term "manager" that we increasingly are using. Thus, the man responsible for running a small A & P store is called a "manager," although his duties and functions are deliberately routine and repetitive. Even a machine — a computer — performing what are called "routines that exercise control" has recently been described as a "manager."

At times the term management takes on a definitely anti-humanist tone. Thus, recently, I saw a full page ad announcing that a Management Manual is now available, a do-it-yourself course in manipulating human beings, including instruction in the use of what is called "the needle as an executive tool." Then, too, we observe the use of the term "human engineering," often with the inference that human beings can be handled with the impersonality and the precision with which engineers measure and handle inanimate materials.

The term management is also applied to a wide range of detailed chores within large-scale enterprises: keeping records of invoices, stock status, customer records, billing, and so on and on. For a time the term "scientific management" was widely current; an engineer with a stop watch analyzing the performance of human beings in an effort to make those human beings more nearly conform to the functioning of machines, rather than devising machines that would more nearly conform to the nature of man.

And so, over the last quarter century particularly, it seems to me, a great, one might say a noble concept, that of the manager as an inspirer and a leader of men, has been given so many meanings that a redefinition of the role of the *manager as leader* seems to me in order. In any case, this is what I shall attempt as the theme of these lectures. This is not to say that the concept of the manager's function in relatively routine tasks has not been useful and certainly does not continue to be useful and essential. But efficiency and control as the manager's function are hardly adequate as things stand in the world today; essential, but hardly inspiring.

In these lectures, I shall have relatively little to say, partly because of limitations of time, of those techniques for getting relatively routine or important functional tasks done more efficiently and of methods of organization for doing these workaday tasks. Of such jobs I have had to do my share, and still do, in my long experience in the management of public and private enterprises. These tasks have included improvements in program evaluation, personnel techniques, improved fact finding and record keeping methods, innovation in organization, the marketing of products, and the rest. These are indeed important aspects of the managerial life.

But now it is a broader concept of the manager as a leader of men and as a do-er that more nearly fits the needs of the crisis areas that confront us all: the areas of violence and war, of widespread hunger, of filthy streams, of poisoned air, of cities that are unlivable and need to be rebuilt, of educational and medical services, outmoded, that must be retooled, of poverty that brutalizes and must be overcome, of bitterness and violence between black and white people — and so on down the long and stern agenda of crises that challenge this generation of men.

As to all these great on-going ventures of mankind, it is my profound conviction—and the theme of these Lectures—that it is the manager as leader who must become the central figure. If my conviction about the broader role of the manager seems far too sanguine to you, I enter the plea of Montaigne when he wrote "there are authors whose purpose is to tell what has happened. Mine, if I could attain it, would be to talk about what *could happen*," and I would add "what with vision and daring and imagination and hardheadedness can be *made to happen*." To discuss so broad a subject adequately, obviously requires more than these three Lectures — plus the criticism and discussion of them which I hope will ensue. So I offer these remarks on the managerial life as a *preface* only, a preface to a much needed re-examination of the human rather than the narrower, technical side of the modern manager's function in the great social-risk ventures of contemporary life.

I have chosen to talk about this function, this art of getting things done in venture areas for a number of reasons. Benjamin Fairless, in whose memory we gather here, devoted most of his life to management. Of many, perhaps most of you who will hear these lectures here, or read them perhaps, the same can be said. Moreover, the life of the manager is the life I have myself lived for the past thirty years in large public business enterprises and for some years now in private business. One who has the instinct of the manager in him is likely to talk about what he knows from his own experience. In any case, firsthand experience is my only important credential to discuss so broad a subject. But the central reason for choosing as a theme the new concept of the manager is, I think, the crucial importance, today — and tomorrow — of the manager's function in getting things done in these great critical areas of this swiftly changing world.

I've used the term "critical areas," and the term "critical" is not simply rhetorical. The blunt fact is that despite twenty years of intense effort in economic and social development, and expenditure of vast amounts of money and application of brains, the world is facing the risk of a major debacle. The explosive gap between the rich and the very poor nations is wider than ever. A failure to narrow this gap might well destroy the foundation for a peaceful world and the greatest hope of modern times: to bring the peoples of the world more closely together.

Only five years ago, the sixties were named hopefully by President Kennedy as the Decade of Development. Will the seventies become the Decade of Debacle? To help prevent this becomes a major challenge to those of us who lead the managerial life.

In describing this particular crisis area I have used strong language. But those most active in carrying hardheaded responsibilities to prevent such a calamity speak in even stronger terms. For example, Mr. George Woods, the great banker and international public servant who heads the World Bank: he is not given to rhetoric for its own sake, nor does he casually push a panic button. But only a few months ago he used these words to describe the gravity of this crisis area of development: "Today, the disparity between the living standards of a prosperous fraction of mankind and the rest of humanity is a gulf that separates the two; *but tomorrow it may swallow up both rich and poor* in political strife and economic chaos." (My italics.)

The role and function of the manager is directly relevant to an examination of this particular threat of a debacle of world-wide development among a number of the crises areas that I propose to discuss.

The heart of the modern managerial task is to close the gap

between man's goals and the fulfillment of those goals; to make practical in men's daily lives the discoveries of the scientist and the techniques of the engineer; to translate into reality the visions and dreams of poets and artists; to bring to actual fruition in men's lives the aspirations of social reformers, the theories and concepts of scholars and economists, the stirrings in the hearts of the compassionate, the desperate need of the hungry, the shelterless, the sick and the heavy laden.

This chasm between what men want and what they have or even seriously hope they can have has always been a wide gap indeed. In the world of today the gap between goals and realization of those goals is wider than at any time in all of history. For never before — in this country and the world over — have the minds of men been so stirred with a ferment of specific wants and desires and demands — and I might add of profound fears and hates. It is these wants and demands — and forebodings and hatreds — that have produced a state of excitement, of tension, of revolutionary and often violent turbulence all over the world. This human turbulence is the prime characteristic of these days in which we live. It must be, I think, the main point of reference in assessing the manager's role.

As a setting for my discussion of the new concept of the manager, I invite you to take a hurried view of man's unprecedented *needs,* many of them here in our own country, and also of our amazing *technical* competence to meet them. Let me quickly tick off a list of some of these crisis areas:

Two-thirds of the world hungry and undernourished. World food production stagnating. World food technology at the highest level in all history.

Bloodshed, rioting and gunfire in the streets of American cities, spurred on by joblessness, squalor and mutual hatred between white and black citizens of the same "developed" country.

All the major streams and lakes of America horribly polluted.

Population increases in the world, and even in our own country, that in another generation can threaten world peace.

The major urban areas of the world — America's included

fifteen

— becoming increasingly unmanageable as decent places to work and to live.

In education, technical methods unheard of even a decade ago ready at hand, yet qualified teachers — our largest body of employment — in short supply.

The very air we breathe, in many urban centers, becoming increasingly foul, to the point of hazard to health.

This list could be extended almost indefinitely: housing, highways, hospitals, and on and on.

The world's *needs* are many; they are prodigious. The technical means at hand to meet them are almost unlimited. There is no lack either, goodness knows, of the articulation of these goals, of eloquent concepts of great revolutionary change. No lack of phrase-makers, no lack of theorists and theories. No lack of institutes, conferences, foundations, research grants to scholars and students. Reports and surveys pour out until we are inundated.

But what about the do-ers, the managers, those who must translate these aspirations, these wants and demands, these unending reports into something tangible in men's lives? Their function, it seems to me, is not too well understood; even by the do-ers themselves.

I suggest to you that under the blowtorch of necessity the function of the do-er, the manager, must be far broader, more comprehensive and more sensitive to the human personality than anything we now know.

The managerial function — whether in private business or public affairs — is too often defined and practiced as solely that of administration — that is, of unifying and weaving together the separate skills and knowledge of technicians and professions. Only rarely is there recognition of dynamic management's chief art — providing the understanding and the inspiration by which men are moved to action. Management's primary skill, in my view, is human, not technical, and therefore the manager must be measured broadly in terms of human personality, the intangible qualities of leadership.

What is the heart of the broad managerial process? I might put it in these words: management requires a humanist outlook on life rather than merely mastery of technique. It is based on the capacity for understanding of individuals and their motivations, their fears, their hopes, what they love and what they hate, the ugly and the good side of human nature. It is an ability to move these individuals, to help them define their wants, to help them discover, step by step, how to achieve them.

The art of management in these terms is a high form of leadership, for it seeks to combine the act — the getting of something done — with the meaning behind that act. The manager-leader would combine in one personality the robust, realistic quality of the man of action with the insight of the artist, the religious leader, the poet, who explain man to himself, who inspire man to great deeds and incredible stamina. The man of action alone, nor the man of contemplation alone, will not be enough in the situations we now confront; these two qualities together are required to meet the world's need for leadership.

As we all see so clearly, the world is changing, and so, therefore, is management changing, more rapidly and more completely than we can fully realize. The manager who hasn't had a new idea in twenty, or even in ten years, who isn't able, by temperament, to jettison most of the ideas of what management leadership consisted of a decade ago, may be as much an anachronism as the prairie schooner or the crossbow in this risky world. Large-scale business, we know, has changed almost beyond recognition, becoming rapidly multi-national and world-wide. The change in government activities is equally rapid and startling, even to the joining with business in a venture in the heavens — Comsat — and soon deep under the sea as well. Europe is far along toward being an economic unit; Latin America begins to follow that example of economic unification. Eastern Asia, the richest of all regions in resources and most numerous in people, is on the way to changing the strategic balance of power and of influence, so that it will be almost unrecognizable in a decade or so.

In the face of such change upon change, managers and management concepts of even ten years ago are also changing. To seek to learn the essence, the basic essentials of the new management in a changing world is therefore an imperative. And these will not be found, I predict, by too great preoccupation with attractive and ingenious mathematical and systems analysis techniques. For the subject of management is man; the objective of management is the moving of man's mind and will and imagination.

It is worth reminding ourselves that management does not really exist. It is a word, an idea. Like science, like government, like engineering, management is an abstraction. But managers exist. And managers are not abstractions; they are men, they are human beings. Particular and special kinds of human beings. Individuals with a special function: to lead and move and bring out the latent capabilities — and dreams — of other human beings.

It is important that we describe and identify these human beings, these managers. This we can do only by recognizing the nature of the demands made upon them as leaders, the pressures they are subjected to by their task of leadership of other men. And consequently the kind of human resources the manager-leader must possess and draw upon, and how those resources, those human talents, make these leaders different from other leaders, leaders who are, let's say, superior poets, or ironworkers, or teachers. These manager-leaders we shall find *are* different from other men, because of their different, their distinctive function. But the basic fact is that though different, they still are *men*.

This I believe, and this my whole life's experience has taught me: the managerial life is the broadest, the most demanding, by all odds the most comprehensive and the most subtle of all human activities. And the most crucial.

May I repeat that the concept of the manager as leader and mover of men I here describe is not one confined to the tasks of production or distribution or of technology. And whether in private enterprise or governmental activity, the areas of which I speak are areas of urgency, of high social risk, and call for the kind of manager-leader equipped by personal characteristics to cope with them.

We are certainly not without many examples of what the

managerial kind of leadership can do in areas of social entrepreneurship. That kind of leadership is natural for a manage-
ment-oriented man, since the goal is not speculation nor rhetoric nor surveys nor concepts, but *action,* by *people.*

Take as examples the rebuilding of the heart of Pittsburgh,
and the abatement of your smoke problem. Those who brought
these things to pass (and it's been a brilliant civic achievement)
were men with a certain spirit and skill in leadership, and a
standing in the community among their fellows. So also in the
rebuilding of the center of Philadelphia or Boston. The list of
reassuring instances in America of what leadership can do to
bring about not just more surveys, but action, is an impressive
one. It will take this kind and quality of civic leadership, and
not alone good engineering or technology, which of course
will be needed, or federal or state legislation, which we can see
will be needed, to save our resources and therefore our future
as a nation.

It throws a good deal of light, in my mind at least, on my
thesis to ask: Why is it that community A moves ahead, while
community B, with the same or better economic advantages of
transport or natural resources and so on, languishes, and even
stagnates?

The answer turns mostly on a difference between the quality
of leadership in those communities. In one community, there
are people-movers, leaders with a managerial bent, people
who provide a special kind of vitality to the community, and
who have a willingness, a necessity even, to give of themselves.
And to give of one's self is the ultimate hallmark of the kind of
leadership that gets things done. Not only gets things done, but
makes for greatness. The greatness of Athens in the days of her
glory as a world force, writes Edith Hamilton in her beautiful
little book, *The Echo of Greece,* "showed what miracles can be
brought about when people willingly work together for the
good of all."* She continues: "Every Athenian as a matter of
course gave time and effort to building and lifting up the
common life. Thucydides makes Pericles say, 'We are a free
democracy . . . We do not allow absorption in our own affairs

*Edith Hamilton, *The Echo of Greece,* p. 30.

nineteen

to interfere with participation in the city's. We regard the man who holds aloof from public affairs as useless; nevertheless we yield to none in independence of spirit and complete self-reliance.' "

To evoke, in our own time, something of this spirit is a part of the managerial function as I have here sought to redefine it, a part of a concept of the function of the manager as leader.

What is true of communities is to a degree true of great private businesses, I think. Of two equally advantaged corporations, one forges ahead with innovations, becomes attractive as a home for enterprising and zestful young men; the other, with virtually the same economic advantages, becomes stodgy, bureaucratic, carried along perhaps by the momentum of its size and its past, its executives little more than temporary caretakers. You know of both kinds. The difference is only rarely a matter of economics; it is almost invariably the difference between the kind of human beings involved.

And so I say our basic problems are human problems. The managers, in the sense in which I use the word in this discussion, are not a specialized professional group, nor are they a self-anointed elite. I speak of a quality of human personality which enables a man to move others to act. And it has been my experience that these manager-leaders are *not* to be found *only* among the chief executives of large companies, or generals, or high public officials; they are, happily, to be found — if one knows how to seek them and to recognize them and to develop them — they are to be found in almost every small community, even some of the most primitive villages in which I've worked in Asia and Latin America; in almost every group of people where a serious and grave venture is to be undertaken, small or large, public or private.

I think the most heartening experience of my life has been to discover how rich and varied are the resources of leadership in what might at first glance seem unlikely places. The Southeastern United States thirty years ago certainly did not appear to the casual observer as a place where local leadership would exist. This proved *not* to be the case; quite the contrary. As year after year I went from town to town on my job in the Tennessee Valley, I found an extraordinary capacity for citizen managerial leadership in improving the school system, say, or in safeguarding local power systems from cheap and corrosive politics, or in strengthening hospital care or local or state government, or promoting community facilities essential for healthy industrial growth. These local leaders, whether in city or country, had the essential ingredient of the managerial leader: the capacity to recognize and stimulate other potential leaders.

In my work overseas in recent years, in Latin America and Asia particularly, I have encountered some of the finest managerial leadership talents I have ever known. The failure fully to recognize potential leadership talent, and the inattention to motivating these able people, seems to me a grave defect, accounting in large measure for the faltering progress in economic development in the underdeveloped countries.

In calling for broad managerial leadership I am not asking that we wait for a new race of supermen, a new elite. No; rather I am convinced that there already exists an enormous resource of management, as I have defined it; however, it remains to be more fully tapped, to be nurtured, motivated, encouraged, indeed liberated. As one example, we need to draw into management, both in private enterprise and in public activities, young people of the kind who bring their enthusiasm, their dedication, their human skills of empathy and leadership to the Peace Corps — but this time not for an interlude of two years or so but as the basis for a career in business or in government. Such young people do exist. And yet all too few are drawn into enterprises that call upon these personal qualities.

It is of the nature of leadership that it reproduces and engenders itself over and over again. The leader must be able to recognize leadership potential in others, he must be able to help bring it forth, to enlarge the vision of other men so that their faith and excitement are aroused. But before he can accomplish this essential act of developing human capabilities, he must see clearly that *this* is the most crucial part of his task. If he considers it incidental or secondary, then he will perform it in an incidental or secondary way. Only if he sees it as primary — if the concept of management which he holds has this as the chief element, whether in a village or a small town or in a great city or in a great company — will he go to the heart of the managerial life which is developing leadership in himself as well as in others. This is an act I have witnessed time and again, perhaps the most inspiring of all, more so than seeing a great dam rising in a mountain gorge, or a giant factory in operation: that of observing and participating in the liberation of human energies.

The essential mark of a successful new manager is that he understands the nature of his function — the kind of job he has, what it will demand of him, the broad range of personal response it must evoke from him, this job which is unlike any other in the world. He must, in short, know what he is. If he cannot interpret himself, then he cannot perform his most important function to others — that is, of interpreting to these others what is going on in their lives, how it could be changed — cannot, therefore, create this community of excitement which produces human results. This concept of the pioneering manager in the urgent and most consequential jobs of the world must be fully understood first by the managers themselves; for a limited technical concept, a concept of conventional management, of slide rule or operations analysis expertise, of old-fashioned stop watch "efficiency," will lead, I fear, to human failure.

We Americans often fail to distinguish between technical "success," and achievement in the more subtle fields of human leadership. The technical man can succeed absolutely because his work is susceptible of a beginning and of an end, of completion. A bridge or a factory is built, a chemical process proves itself and succeeds. But the new manager working with people will fail, by standards of technical measurement, even when he achieves a partial objective. For this function there is no "completion." So we believe we are exporting our success (what we call our technical "know-how") when we send successful agricultural or industrial technicians abroad, and we are puzzled and hurt when so often they seem to "fail." But when the problems they face are largely human, not technical problems, of course they are likely to fail; as technicians they may be the wrong men for human problems.

The newer concept of the manager is the expression in another form of democracy's basic concept of man himself, of man as the center, the object of all our efforts; our belief in his capacity for growth, the measure of our faith in man and in his future.

November 3, 1966

The following are questions put to Mr. Lilienthal by members of the audience, and his answers.

Q. Can leadership be taught?

A. I don't think so, not directly and self-consciously. That is, I don't think one could have a course — "Leadership 14." But I think it can be taught in the sense that we have imaginative teaching of what we call the humanities, history, biography, the lives of other men. Experiences of the human race do have a distinct bearing on the teaching of leadership.

Q. In 1964 you said that generation of power from the atom was a menace and a failure. Have you changed your mind?

A. I think it's a little early to be too sure about the atom; we need to know what the price of uranium is going to be ten years from now, compared to other fuels. But the main point I made was that the earlier euphoria about the atom as a virtually costless source of power was a mistake; that it's not magic; that power from the atom will not be so cheap that it needn't be metered. To that extent I think I was correct, and I think there now is pretty general agreement on those points.

But I also said that when the time came when atomic energy would be competitive, that is to say would cost no more and have no dangerous hazards greater than power from other fuels, that the private utilities and the public utilities and the manufacturing industries would see to it that the equipment was made and used; that the Atomic Energy Commission and the Joint Congressional Committee on Atomic Energy were not necessary to prod industry.

twenty-three

One most impressive change has come about, however, and one that I hoped would, but at the time when I spoke made me feel rather low about atomic energy, when the problems of hazards of radioactivity had not been treated with the seriousness that it seemed to me they require. This technical job is an unpleasant one, of minimizing the hazards from handling of spent radioactive materials. It was handed off to just whomever would take it, not to the ablest technical outfits. Perhaps my prodding about hazards did some good. If a preoccupation with preventing catastrophes from radioactivity continues, then atomic energy may be definitely on its way.

Q. Your definition of the manager sounds too broad. For example, what is or is there any difference between a manager and a political leader who also has the capability and insight of perceiving people's minds, and also the ability to move them?

A. I've taken a very fine old word — manager —, a word that has some two thousand years of history back of it, and tried to resurrect it and give it the broad meaning that I've suggested. Perhaps it is too broad a meaning, as you suggest. But the managerial function is one that can hardly be described except in broad terms.

Q. Do you believe our educational system today is developing the kinds of managers or leaders of whom you speak?

A. Yes and no. I think the concept of university education that is exemplified by Carnegie is most likely to produce this kind of manager. For here at Carnegie you see a world in which technology and engineering are important indeed; also a world in which the arts and humanities are of equal or even greater importance. And to be able to build a university on these two concepts as you are, is, I think, the right direction for education in terms of leadership.

II. Management leadership
as a humanist art

II. Management leadership as a humanist art

The central motif of these three lectures is an effort to redefine the role and function of the modern manager. The manager's function, basically, is to get things done, to make things happen. But to make things happen by virtue of his special human qualities: his capacity to lead and inspire and move other men to act. In the opening lecture, I proposed such a redefinition, calling it the highest form of the managerial function and suggesting that that function be regarded as a humanist rather than merely a technical skill.

The highest and truest managerial function is leadership in the crisis areas of human life today, areas in which the decisive need is for those human qualities which managerial talent at its best exhibits: the capacity to get things done by an understanding of people and a capacity to persuade and to move them. In this lecture I pursue this theme further, and will also seek to apply this redefinition to some of the acute issues in our own country, such as water and air pollution, urban elephantiasis, and other pressing American issues.

The importance of the manager's function is not something new, not something arising out of the coming of modern industry and government. The nature of the function changes, sometimes radically, as the society of which it is a central fact changes. I suggest that it is worth our while to take a look at the history of the managerial function, to give us a better perspective on the present and the future. So I shall divert your attention momentarily for a quick glance at that history.

I spoke of the necessity for perspective. But obtaining perspective is not an easy thing. I had a lesson in perspective from a little old lady in the mountains of western North Carolina, the wife of the keeper of a rather primitive ferry across a stream in that part of the country. A group of engineers and I from the TVA were on our way one evening to the site of a new dam; we knew that we had a stream to cross in that ferry. But we got to talking and didn't pay much attention, and the first thing we knew we'd driven our car right smack in the middle of this river; it took quite a while to get it pulled out. I was delegated to go up to the ferry keeper's house and tell him what we thought of him. So I knocked on the door and a sweet little old lady said, "What's the matter?" And I said, "What's the matter? We just drove into the river. You keep a ferry here. Why don't you put up a big sign, 'River Ahead,' so a fellow would know." And she said, "God a-mighty, mister, if you couldn't see the river, you couldn't see the sign."

Beginning about ten years ago the management company which I head has been deeply involved in a vast area of the Mesopotamian plains in Persia — or Iran, as it's often called — the eastern part of the Fertile Crescent of ancient days; the land that in the Old Testament is called Elam. There we have been responsible for devising a program for the restoration of a very large region, including responsibility for the design and erection of one of the world's highest dams, of irrigation canals, the working out of new land cropping patterns, the training of Persian farmers in agriculture and in health, to restore the land's productivity and the people's health; and also concerned with electric power in large quantities, so as to bring that region into the industrialized 20th Century. In this huge enterprise the modern manager's function is a central part of the task. But the point I wish to make now is that thousands of years ago, in this very area where civilization is said to have had its beginnings, it was managers who made that beginning of civilization a reality.

In a recently scholarly work, Professor McNeill of the University of Chicago refers to the very beginnings of organized agriculture and community life on this planet, which occurred, he and other scholars say, in Mesopotamia thousands of years ago. Then he has this to say about the role of the manager in that dawn of civilization (I am now quoting from Professor McNeill's book, The Rise of the West): "Irrigation was vital to early civilization because it put the production of a regular agricultural surplus easily within the reach of primitive farmers." I think if Professor McNeill had been working with primitive farmers, as I have, he would have stricken the word "easily"; but it certainly put it within the reach of farmers. "Even more important," he goes on to say, "by requiring very massive coordination of social effort, irrigation facilitated the creation of a social engine for the concentration of surplus foods *in the hands of a managerial group.* And once the body of managers had established its right to collect a part of the farmers' surplus crops, growing numbers of men could be employed not only to dig canals, but also to elaborate the cult of the god, to undertake military enterprises, and to specialize as craftsmen, artists, or musicians: to create, in short, a civilization. . . . Without the necessity of organized, large-scale collective effort on canals and dikes," Dr. McNeill continues, "a managerial group could not establish control over whatever surplus may have been available."* (My italics)

So I think it can be said that the managerial function has indeed remote historic antecedents. But in some parts of the world, that role is now outmoded. Only ten years ago, when our company first began work in Persia on the same Mesopotamian plains of which Professor McNeill writes, the managerial group, the large landowners, were exercising essentially an autocratic managerial function and authority over the people on the land and the fruits of their labor. The peasants, many of them, were still using methods less productive than those in the days of Hammurabi, centuries and centuries ago. In the past ten years, the beginning of a new kind of managerial role has come to that ancient beginning point of civilization. A very different concept of the manager is emerging in Persia, taking the place of the landowner as manager.

In our own country, and within the memory of many of my generation, the manager's function was also essentially an autocratic one. That function in the early decades of this century in America was generally not leadership by persuasion or inspiration or participation, but by authority and by command. It is worthwhile to remind ourselves of this older concept of the manager's function to help give perspective to the new.

---

*W. H. McNeill, *The Rise of the West.* Mentor edition (1965), pp. 80, 81.

As a youth I lived for a time in Gary, Indiana, where only a few years before the United States Steel Corporation had established a great steel complex on the shores of Lake Michigan. A new city, Gary, was created essentially by the decision of one strong and very able man, Judge Elbert Gary. The hours of labor — seven days a week and twelve hours a day — the rate of pay and the conditions of living of the labor force were matters the manager's group decided. As I learned at firsthand two or three years later, as a cub reporter on a Gary newspaper, the political life of Gary also was largely determined by the managerial group of U.S. Steel. There was no need to get the approval of anyone, whether the question was conditions of safety or health in the mills, or the educational system provided for the city of Gary — which incidentally was an unusually good one.

Gary and its new mills represented the usual pattern of the managerial role of those days. All over America, at that time, it was this power to decide, often benevolently, often ruthlessly, but always without having to consult its work force, or to heed public opinion, or seek to persuade or consult any public authority, that wrought a kind of physical miracle in our land: the creation of America's industrial sinews. And just as the managerial group of ancient Mesopotamia made possible the development of a higher standard of living, of cultivation of the arts, and the capacity to defend against enemies, so those early days in our own history have made possible the kind of developed and developing country we have become, and will increasingly become.

But times have changed since the early decades of this century, and with time the very nature of the managerial function has changed. Contrast Gary and the establishment of that steel mill more than 50 years ago with the decision of the Bethlehem Steel Co. to erect a steel complex at Burns Creek on Lake Michigan, not far from Gary. The function of the Bethlehem managers in the 1960's was not simply to decide, but to persuade, to lead and move the minds of many people, at every step, on almost every conceivable subject. For example, some people thought that the Bethlehem mills at Burns Harbour would destroy an important scenic and recreational resource, the sand dunes that in Judge Gary's day were considered by most people as simply wasteland, their use of no possible concern to anyone but U.S. Steel. The impairment of a scenic resource is wholly unrelated to the economics and the technical aspects of steel making. Yet it became a major public issue in recent years, widely debated in Congress and in the press, and before the Bethlehem mill could be built many people had to be persuaded on this issue.

Or take water and air pollution: When I was a young man in Gary the ovens and furnaces poured great wastes into the atmosphere. Lake Michigan's waters were used, in huge quantities, in steel making with scant thought by the managerial group of the effect on the purity of Lake Michigan for water supply and recreation. Judge Gary, I daresay, would have been aghast at the notion that health officials or the general public must be consulted about how that mill was run. Yet today Bethlehem (and U.S. Steel also, I'm sure) has invested large sums to minimize pollution of the air and water, and they are proud enough of their public outlook to advertise this fact widely. Keeping air and water pollution at minimum levels has become a part of the modern concept of the manager's function, and persuading the public and the health authorities that its efforts are effective is no longer considered an outrageous invasion of the function of the manager. This change in outlook is a revolution in managerial concepts.

But there are other parts of the world — notably in the underdeveloped countries, and in some parts of Europe as well — where the manager's function is still that of dictation, and where the manager is typically not a leader but an order-er. This we sometimes forget as a changed America struggles with the problems of communicating with and understanding and doing business with some of these countries that are still living in that world we have left behind.

The nature of the manager's job in the days of Judge Gary was different because the society was different. What constituted a successful "job of doing," i.e., of management, was utterly different than it is today. Driving the job through, regardless, was the test of the manager.

The modern manager in our American society is a quite different kind of man because the society is so changed it is hardly recognizable. Now the modern manager must and usually does take the broad public interest and public opinion into account. The successful manager of today needs a range of understanding, of stamina and above all ability to lead and persuade and motivate and induce agreement beyond anything ever laid on the shoulders of any manager in all history. What the manager, particularly in what I've called the risk areas, the crisis areas, *must* know, has become all encompassing. The specialist and the expert must know some things intimately; the new manager that I am describing, to perform well, must know almost everything well.

The manager must have knowledge of technical and scientific developments of many kinds. If he is engaged in industry, he must consult and persuade labor organizations. If his responsibilities reach overseas — and with the internationalization of business they are likely to — he must have a grasp of foreign affairs, be aware of the culture and the sensibilities of those in the countries in which his managerial function is exercised. If he takes on foreign partners, as is becoming increasingly true in large enterprises, he must have knowledge of business conditions and business ethics, of public opinion and cultures in those countries too. And here at home, such intense social and human issues as providing economic opportunities for Negroes become part of the range of understanding he must somehow have at his command.

But far more than broad knowledge or great skills in harmonizing divergent interests is demanded in my concept of the new manager. To be a mediator or conciliator between people or interests is not the heart of the new managerial function. For the manager, in the great and urgent tasks of manhood, is a man responsible *for making things happen,* in the areas of venture, of social entrepreneurship. He is dealing, under the pressure of events, with other human beings. And, therefore, whatever the particular subject matter, he must possess the personal, emotional, and imaginative qualities that move other people, that enable him to motivate and induce them not only to agreement *but to action.*

In the past fifteen years or so, a great deal of emphasis has been put on surveys, on great masses of "facts," or feasibility studies, and prefeasibility studies and studies of studies, on systems analysis and analysis of systems analysis, on "Plans" (with a capital "P"). Clearly there is great value in such studies, if done with good sense. But the degree of confidence some people tend to put in their magic is misplaced. This intense preoccupation with survey-itis grows, I think in some cases, out of a lack of awareness that it is action by people, by individuals, that is central to the management function. And to move and motivate people, the manager must be a man who has a good understanding of them. This kind of leadership calls for a human capacity to interpret the desires and emotions of others, and to convey a realistic picture of these desires to others.

Recently Secretary Gardner, former head of the Carnegie Corporation (a foundation devoted to education), and now the head of a very sprawling department of our government, Health, Education and Welfare, referred to what he called the "new twists" being added to the modern art of what he called "how to reach decisions without really deciding," the devising of "elaborate statistical systems, cost-account systems, information-processing systems, hoping that out of them will come unassailable support for one course of action or another." We must beware lest we breed a narrow stratum of people who are smart and facile — and insensitive to the springs of action within human beings; insensitive to human emotion.

If I were asked what I have learned, or what I think I have learned, about the managerial process over the past thirty years and about the dynamics of change with which the managerial life must deal, I would put it this way:

The greatest of all resources, the indispensable ones, are the energies of individuals. Therefore, it is a key task of managerial leadership to recognize the existence of these often unused or partially used human talents, energies, and imagination. In short, the full release of human energy is the central purpose and function of the manager at all levels, in private as well as civic enterprises.

With this concept of what the managerial process is all about, at its core and center, naturally I look with the greatest of skepticism at efforts to eliminate or minimize elements of human diversity — the difference between people — to eliminate this from economic life or political life. And, therefore, I look with reservations upon those instances I have observed, and it seems to me they're increasing, of an uncritical or euphoric effort to use mathematical techniques and models for the broader aspects of the management process. Or, I may add, to use them in military strategy. Indeed, my reservations are even greater about some of the newly risen priesthood, the civilian professional military strategist who confidently applies various forms of impersonal mathematics of systems analysis to the basically human problem we call warfare, or the equally human and essentially nontechnical issue of disarmament.*

The raising to a new level of excitement and acuteness of spiritual energies is the ultimate goal of leadership. It was this that glorified the pages of the history of Elizabethan England; it was this that marked the great era of the Spanish and Portuguese explorations and adventures; it was this that built great cathedrals and immortal works of art. It is this same magic of human personality that the new concept of the managerial function brings to the urgent crisis areas of our life today. The farther leadership is separated from the problem of stirring and inspiring and enlarging the capacity of individuals, the farther it wanders from what I believe to be the heart of leadership. It is no wonder that efforts are made in this direction, for this kind

---

*Note the comment of a distinguished British scientist and strategist, Dr. P. M. S. Blackett: "If it is difficult to find legitimate military reasons for the vast number of U.S. nuclear weapons and delivery vehicles, it is clear that military arguments alone are not likely to be dominant in U.S. discussion of a possible drastic first step toward nuclear disarmament. This is widely admitted in the U.S., where the impediments to disarmament are *being seen more and more as economic, political and emotional in origin* rather than as based on operational military considerations." (My italics) Essay on "Steps Toward Disarmament" in *The Strategy of World Order*, ed. Falk and Mendlovitz. World Law Fund, 1966.

of leadership of people is a highly subtle thing; too great preoccupation in some quarters with computers, with electronic data processing, the glamourizing of what are at best tools, and very good tools, seems to be an understandable effort to escape from the necessity for sensitivity to emotional and political factors, to escape from the diverse qualities of individuals and the demands of human judgments.

I was reading last night the first volume of the memoirs of Harold Macmillan, former Prime Minister of England. He referred to an instance that illustrates this point. At the close of World War I, Britain had the problem of demobilizing one of the most heroic civilian armies that had ever been assembled to protect that island. And the job of an orderly demobilization of these men, who wanted to get home and out of the Army, as civilians who are soldiers do, was turned over to planners. And they came up with a plan which Macmillan said had everything to be said for it — in terms of logic. But anyone with any sensitivity about people would have recognized that this plan would be regarded as unfair, and "unfair" in the United Kingdom is a very ugly word; unfair to individuals. The plan had to be junked, and Winston Churchill, who did have a sense of what's fair and what isn't fair, threw it out and devised a simpler one that appealed to the fairness of the average Briton in the Army. So serious was this reaction to the logic of this plan that the historic Brigade of Grenadiers almost had a mutiny. This is what happens when one carries rationality too far, overriding the nature of the human being.

If our purpose is to lead, and stimulate, and stir, and release the full scope of their latent talents, computerizing human beings will not work. One can manipulate human beings in great mobs and crowds — they can be manipulated by force. But this is not leadership and it is not good management any more than it is good political philosophy or economic philosophy.

The manager in the area of great events is capable by the nature of his function and his personality to see what others aren't in a position to see. He sees qualities and capacities in other people that they themselves cannot see, is able to interpret other people to themselves. These qualities consitute a force, a stimulus that moves others to action, action that is understood and comprehended by those who are acting.

One man sees in a block of stone an inert piece of rock. A sculptor sees in that stone a figure that he can shape from the stone, into what may become an immortal object. The sculptor's act is creative. No less an act of creation is that of the manager, who sees in human desires, loves, hates, aspirations, the materials from which to create something that did not exist before, whether it is in the development of a community, the increase in food, or the alleviation of tensions. These human materials are more complex, volatile, changeable, difficult to deal with, than anything that even the artist faces. And the results fully as creative, and fully as consequential. The full beauty of the creative process in managerial life appears when people say, "Yes, that's the way it is, or that's the way it could be," just as people instinctively recognize truths which artists project through painting, through poetry, through music.

But what distinguishes the manager as leader from other kinds of leadership is this: that it is the manager's function to get things done, sometimes "impossible" things, urgent, critical things. And this he must do under the gun of necessity, sometimes under the gun almost literally; for of some of the problems of the world the alternative to a measure of success is violence, bloodshed, and revolution, or in some parts of the world, the shadow of famine.

I reserve for my concluding lecture a statement of my views on the art of getting things done overseas, in the deteriorating picture of economic development in the poorer countries. For the remaining portion of this lecture, I turn, primarily, to contemporary cases in our own country that illustrate the nature of the manager-leader role.

I put at the top of a list of such cases of need for managerial leadership, the need to open wider the doors of human and economic opportunity to our Negro citizens; this may indeed prove to be the most explosive, the most urgent, and the most difficult of all, and in which the broad gauge comprehension of the manager-leader may prove decisive.

thirty-five

The progressive physical congestion and deterioration of the *quality* of life that men can lead in our great urban centers should certainly be on such a list.

Air pollution has reached the point in many cities where it can no longer be ignored, or treated as a mere sporadic nuisance. Nor is the poisoning of the atmosphere any longer a problem of certain big cities; it has become, in many places, a regional problem of great magnitude. Nor will the mere passing of legislation, a common American way of sweeping a problem under the bed, be enough. Human managerial leadership is the essential ingredient.

This point, I think, is well illustrated by an article in a recent (September 27, 1966) issue of the *New York Times*. A report from Los Angeles began in this way:

"In a large city in the Middle West a few weeks back, a nationally respected air pollution official concluded a disquisition on the nation's mounting smog problem by abruptly sweeping aside his sliderule, charts and tabulations and exclaiming:

" 'That's the official story. Now do you want to hear the truth?

" 'The truth is that the critical ingredient in smog simply is politics. By that I mean people and their instruments of government, and their attitudes about a community problem.

" 'We know how to cure smog. It's not unduly difficult or expensive. The problem is getting the people in the community to support a cleanup program.' "

In some of the vast arid regions of the earth with which, because of my work, I am familiar, water has for centuries been the difference between life and death. Not so in America, with its abundance — or so we thought. But no longer is this quite true. Hanging over much of America is the spectre of diminishing supplies and unbelievably filthy pollution of many of our greatest rivers and bodies of water: the Hudson, the Potomac, the Delaware, Lake Erie, Lake Michigan, and so on.

I suggest we spend a few minutes examining the question of water supply and pollution, as a way of illustrating the points I have tried to make earlier about the strategic and essential role of the human factor in getting things done, in this case, water supply and purity.

What are the main obstacles?

Clearly not the absence of a broad concept. We've had a broad concept dealing with the waters of America since Theodore Roosevelt's commission almost fifty years ago, and then these were set out with great literary skill and compelling technical support in the Morris L. Cooke Report of 1950. We did have a concept and we had technology. But nothing *happened*, and it is *what can be made to happen* that is the manager's chief concern. The pollution of rivers and the improvident use of our water resources continued on its way, reports or no reports. Technology and manufacturing facilities to purify polluted water were not lacking in this period. Yet the pollution continued and increased, and increases today.

Suddenly, as if the danger were something quite new, localities and the nation have become aroused, emotionally at least, sufficiently to pass legislation and appropriate very large sums of money. Industries have taken the problem with the greatest seriousness.

Will anything substantial happen now; will those things get done we know how to do but have not done before?

The answer will depend, I suggest, not principally upon technology or finance, although obviously both are involved, but upon that area of affairs which is within the scope of the manager-leader's special ability. In short, the conquering of water pollution is primarily a problem of human response and human agreement, within the communities, within industries, throughout the nation.

A great many people and many communities must see pollution as the result of the action of many industries and many municipalities throughout an entire watershed. To pick out a scapegoat here or there will not solve the problem. To clean up a stream at city A or industry B by technical means long since at our disposal will not suffice. The watershed is the smallest practical unit.

Now, to get joint action through an entire watershed requires creation of the awareness of the nature of the problem and a widespread conviction of the need for particular action. It requires the creation and manning of new institutions, participated in by many units in that watershed. Such awareness of the nature of the problem, such a conviction, must be shared by many people and by many institutions, public and private, local and region-wide. Moreover, how the cost is to be paid for, and particularly how the total costs are to be allocated among industries, cities, regions, is a complex question full of the certainty of conflict of opinions and interests. If not resolved by the talents of manager-leaders, experienced and wise in just such matters, the issues could produce a decade of delay and acrimony — and more pollution. Only when we realize the human problems in this area will the dimensions of the managerial task become fully apparent. People generally — and not just their Congressmen or Governors — will have to be persuaded in graphic ways that water pollution does have a very high priority; they will have to be persuaded that the high costs are justified, and, not the least prickly, that those costs are fairly and reasonably shared.

None of this will happen just by passing laws or setting up commissions or appropriating money. It will be the function, I think, of the new manager-leader to evoke a human response, to get others to see those problems as he sees them, and to stimulate the beginnings of a community of excitement about the possibilities that lie in action in this huge task. The foundations will have to be laid not in Washington but within the communities, among civic leaders in private life, in private business and in education. I need only refer to what I said last Thursday about the way in which Pittsburgh and Boston and Philadelphia have shown the way in which civic leaders and civic leadership can make changes which without that kind of leadership are quite impossible. The same thing will be true, I think, with the other problems that communities throughout the country are facing.

How does the manager approach such challenges to social entrepreneurship? On this, let me make one general observation or two.

First, the manager must have a sense of timing, a sense of

what can be done *when;* he must be able to recognize when a situation has reached a point where people are ready to act. Water resources is certainly such a case. In 1950, at the time of the distinguished Cooke Report, the answers were technically clear. But it came at a time when little could be done; and little was done. By 1966 conditions had so worsened that action was possible; it became a time when the manager has a chance to be effective. Action came within the range of the feasible.

Let me divert for a moment from the United States to another part of our Hemisphere. We can see this same sense of timing that marks the manager-leader in the great impetus now being given to a concept long cherished in Latin America, that of economic integration of that vast region of 200 million people. Some of the younger modern leaders of Latin America have been able to create a mood of looking forward to the great things that can come as a result of economic integration. A community of confidence and optimism is coming into being. Without this the manager-leader knows no action can be taken; but with that mood, action can at least come within the range of the feasible. One after another of the new business and political leaders of much of Latin America show clearly — and as a part of my current work in Latin America I see this at first hand — that they begin to sense that the timing is right. This sense of timing is one of the marks of how the broad-gauged manager-leader goes about his function.

Let me repeat what I have said earlier: I am *not* asking that we wait for a new race of supermen, a self-annointed elite, an elite alone capable of filling the high role of leadership I have been trying to describe. My own experience persuades me that there already exists an enormous potential resource of this quality in the primitive villages of Persia or Colombia, or in the small towns of the Tennessee Valley or the Middle West, with which I'm familiar, as well as in large business or governmental organizations. An enormous potential of humanist managerial capacity does exist, and not just at the level of presidents of corporations or generals or great political leaders, but what one can only call natural leaders; men in the neighborhoods and towns and even in the remote villages overseas. My thesis is that this latent capability be more fully recognized, motivated, and liberated.   November 7, 1966

The following are questions put to Mr. Lilienthal by members of the audience, and his answers.

Q.   Can leadership as you conceive it innovate? Is it innate or must it be the result of training? If so, what do you conceive of as a program of training that would be desirable for training the kind of manager that you're talking about?
A.   You certainly couldn't have a formal course in Leadership, where if you got the highest mark you'd be a leader. It isn't that kind of quality.

The emergence of leaders has not followed any single pattern. The kind of leaders that we're talking about are men and women who have convictions, to begin with; who have an outlook on life; who have a philosophy of life. These are not as common as one would think. And whether one has convictions, whether one has a philosophy of life may be the outcome of reading Shakespeare or the Bible or listening to music or looking at a pretty girl; there are many ways in which one gets a feeling about what life's all about. But there are a great many people who not only don't know what life's about, but don't even want to know. Those people will not be leaders. The number of young people of this generation who *do* have convictions I find is surprisingly great.

What I understand to be a current trend, to have people who are technically trained also be committed to the arts and humanities, is one of the best ways of bringing out the latent qualities of leadership.

Q.   With rapid advances in management practices, how can the mature company deal with top management obsolescence?
A.   This is a problem that government has had, and that I suppose churches have among the boards of deacons, and boards of directors have, as well as management itself.

What do you do with people who haven't had a new idea for twenty years and don't propose to have any? And yet who have what in the academic world is called tenure; what in govern-ment is called civil service security? It's the conflict between security and a rapidly moving society.

In some older societies what happened was that if the leader became obsolescent and the neighboring tribe invented a crossbow instead of an arrow and cleaned the place out, that sleepy leader was out of business at the hands of his own group.

But how to deal with this problem in large-scale business seems to me a very puzzling thing. Because men don't appear to become obsolescent in the more obvious ways that machines do. Some of the oldest and most hidebound men I know are fellows in their early forties. One of the most zippy manager-leaders I've known was Gerard Swope, who was pushing and nudging General Electric when he was in his late seventies.

Q. In the era preceding large-scale economic development, whether in Gary, Indiana, or in the plains of Mesopotamia or in the Soviet Union, management by command rather than man-agement by persuasion has generally been the order of the day. Do you regard this as a necessary or important stage of devel-opment, a stage that a country must pass through on the road to participative decision-making?

A. My own answer to that is very simple. I think it is a necessary stage; and I'm glad we're out of it.

Q. 1) Your definition of manager requires a good deal of altruism. Granted that in some cases altruism may be compati-ble with sound business, it hardly seems to be always so. How do you reconcile the profit motive with your definition of the new manager?

2) Should the modern manager be more responsive to the will of the community than to the will of the stockholders? What is the community responsibility to the stockholder?

A. I won't try to evade these two excellent tough questions by saying that in the long run the stockholder is better off in financial terms if his management is altruistic. Probably true, but that's not really a complete answer.

forty-one

I would rather put it in this way: a company's management should be concerned with its impact upon its community. Good managers are like other good people, they are good men; they have their own standards; they respect themselves, the best of them.

It happens that this good, this sense of responsibility to the community, works out to the financial advantage of the company. But I don't think it ought to be put solely on that basis. The most important thing that has happened in the managerial life in business in my time has been a change in the minds of businessmen. There has been an important change in the way the business community looks at its place in society, its obligation to its employees and to its community.

Now obviously if this viewpoint is carried to the point where the company suffers financial strain, this means the company is on its way out. A business man has to so function that his company is able to stay in business, which means make a profit. But the capacity of larger businesses to earn and earn well against their competitors, has eased so that among larger companies in this growing society, I don't think the old formula that you can't do this because you're robbing the stockholders (who've not seemed to me to be particularly impoverished lately) is any longer the main issue.

I think that the best manager is the one concerned about broad community responsibilities because he believes this is the right thing to do and that increasingly this is taking hold of the mentality of the top management and the middle management of American business.

Q. What do you propose be done to utilize the talents of those possessing latent managerial capabilities that you describe. What can be done to bring disadvantaged groups into positions of managerial responsibility in our own country; or what can be done to bring larger participation in the management of their own affairs by Africans or Asians in underdeveloped countries?

A. The last part of this question I do take up directly and with illustrations out of my experience in the closing lecture.

The first part of the question gives me an opportunity to correct what I'm sure must be in some of your minds; that is, the notion that managerial leadership inheres only in people in a relatively elevated station.

My wife's grandmother's role in leadership in the little Indiana town where she lived, was managerial leadership of a high order. She had no public post or authority. She was not running a company. She had a special human quality, one that made people come to her, enabled her to impress her personality and her viewpoint on others. And in every block, in every precinct, in every town that I've ever known well, there are such people. And to recognize that this is a high order of ability, to encourage it, to recognize it as a distinction, is one of the things we have not done enough of. I think we can start in the grade school with this. There are leaders in the lower grades. We need to identify this quality as a precious thing; perhaps more important than getting straight A's.

III. Overseas development
as a humanist art

III. Overseas development as a humanist art

Why should a man who is as busy as your speaker is running a business take the time and the effort to prepare three full-scale lectures, sweat over them, worry about them? I think it's relevant to the special quality of Carnegie Tech to ask such a question. The answer, in my case at least, is that here, perhaps more than in any education center and in any city of which I have knowledge, there is an opportunity for scientific and technical people to be exposed to the humanities, to the arts, to drama, with a closeness that is rare in any other technical and scientific center. And at the same time you give those who are engaged in liberal arts and non-scientific pursuits a better comprehension of those fields by rubbing elbows, as it were, with scientific and technical people.

We've heard a good deal about the two cultures. Here at Carnegie Tech there is the beginning, I believe, of welding these two cultures together, in an educational institution that sees the two as one.

The most ominous single fact about our contemporary world is that the gap between the poor and the rich nations continues to widen — a weight upon our conscience, a real and a present and a continuous threat to peace. It is ominous and at the same time it presents to mankind the widest door of opportunity, a historic opportunity. The most severe test of the concept of the new manager as leader, which I've tried to describe in the preceding lectures, is whether management, conceived of as a humanist art, can add the decisive factor in speeding the economic and social development of the poorer areas of the world, and begin to close this inhumane and explosive gap.

In any perspective of time a change in this state of affairs is not solely a matter of technology or techniques, nor greatly increased inflow of capital, essential as these are. For the heart of development is increasing the capabilities of people. This has been the theme of preceding lectures; it sums up my own experience here at home in the United States, and in Asia, Latin

America and Africa. The question that I ask that we here consider is this: Can managerial leadership of the kind I have attempted to describe buttress, or help restore, the now endangered and faltering progress of economic development in most of the poorer nations? A quick review of what has been attempted and where things stand today is necessary if we are to judge what the function of the new manager can contribute to economic development.

For twenty years now the World Bank, a U.N. agency, has been struggling with this challenge. Since 1948 the United States has engaged in a series of efforts beginning with President Truman's Point IV program of technical assistance. The United States Development Loan Fund has extended credits to scores of poorer countries. About five years ago President Kennedy hopefully launched the Decade of Development and the Alliance for Progress in Latin America. The United Nations has had a program under the redoubtable Paul Hoffman of Marshall Plan fame. The United Nations Food and Agriculture Organization — the FAO — has had its experts over a good part of the world during a period of many years. European nations have had their own programs. Private business has made substantial investments of money, of men, and of know-how in some of these countries. American foundations have been active on these problems, spending great sums. American construction and consulting firms have blanketed the globe. American universities have created a score or more of international centers for research and for overseas development operations. International conferences on development by the dozen have brought together highly intelligent, or in any case highly articulate, experts. Experts of every kind have provided the poorer countries with advice and passed judgment on what they should and definitely what they should not do.

What has all this come to for the underdeveloped countries — all this sincere effort, these billions of dollars granted or loaned or invested, these volumes of plans and mountains of expert advice or direction? The answer, one must realistically and reluctantly admit, has been grave disappointment and frustration. The gap between the richer and the poorer nations has not been narrowing, but widening.

The generous American public and Congress find the results of development assistance disillusioning — to put it very mildly. With a few notable exceptions the results have grossly disappointed and even antagonized some of the poorer countries. Well-to-do Western nations, some of which have been put on their feet with American funds since the War, have permitted the United States to carry most of the financial burden, a sorry state of affairs, and one that is rightly resented in this country. But the most impressive and I think the most objective judgment of the shortcomings of development come from the World Bank. That body has become the acknowledged leader in the drive for economic development.

The Bank's conclusion appears to be this: Where development is most needed, in the poorest and the most populous regions of the world, it faces a grave threat. To avert a complete collapse requires radical changes in policies of lending and in the quantum of funds flowing into development. It requires, according to the Bank, additional capital from its richer member states and from private business. The minimum needs set by the Bank are of an order of magnitude that is very large, and not likely of early attainment. Moreover, to overcome development inadequacies requires a new look at the "mechanics and techniques" of development, including the professional economists' "model" for the planning of development, so proudly and confidently, I almost said arrogantly, built up over the years.

One of America's most experienced investment bankers, now head of the World Bank, Mr. George Woods, is not given to extremist or alarmist statements. Yet on July 20 of this year Mr. Woods, speaking to a ministerial conference of European nations, described as "ominous" the state of economic development of the poorer countries vis-a-vis the richer, and used these words:

"Looking ahead over the next ten years, where are the threats to international tranquility and order? Are they confined to balance and maintenance of military strength among the most powerful nations? Or to financial questions among the richest?

Or is there also a threat arising from the possibility that, without concerted and adequate help from abroad, a large part of humanity will remain on the ragged edge of subsistence? I believe this is a possibility which presents a real and present danger."

Something must be very wrong. Are the current prevailing concepts of development wrong? Or the manner of their execution over this period of twenty years? Or is the assumption of the Western nations wrong that the poorer nations can ever, by peaceful democratic means, pull themselves closer to the level of living standards of the developed countries?

What are some of those concepts? What have been the chief methods of development in these poorer nations? Finally, what if any, constructive ideas and experience can the new managerial way of thinking contribute? To a necessarily summarized discussion of such broad questions I devote the balance of this discussion.

Since the administration of these countries as colonies became intolerable, or in any case unacceptable, the concept with the longest history and the most respected standing had its origin at Bretton Woods twenty years ago, namely, that the basic need of the underdeveloped nations was capital, and that the lending practice of good, prudent banking could most quickly bring these nations to the point of self-support. The World Bank was the instrument of this concept.

The funds of the Bank were not to be derived solely from tax revenues of the nation-members but principally from private investors in the World Bank's own securities, backed by government guarantees. By this device the private capital markets were open to the World Bank and through the Bank to the underdeveloped countries. Loans to these underdeveloped nations, under this concept, would be made on "bankable" projects. That is, the initiative was put upon the poorer countries to present "projects" that would pass the tests of rigorous "economic justification," including ability of such projects to pay interest and repayment on schedules much like those that a prudent private banker might impose on a private borrower. This "businesslike" approach reassured the American public

forty-nine

and Congress that banking prudence would pay off for the underdeveloped countries and protect the American taxpayer from "give-aways." One mark of confidence in this conventional banking and economic approach was that the bonds of the World Bank in the private capital markets achieved the accolade of a triple A rating among private investors.

The results, as well as the standards applied, were regarded — until very recently indeed — as a great success story. Here was the application to a vital public need of the fruits of private banking good sense. True, not a few of the borrowing nations objected, from time to time, sometimes emphatically, to having bankers overrule their own policies about what their country needed most. But this grumbling was said to underline the superiority of purely economic judgments, backed by the power of the banking purse and the objective judgment of the multinational technical staffs of an international lending agency.

For the countries needing development most urgently, this *conventional banking approach is almost overnight seen to be a failure,* because it is defeating the whole object of development. The Bank itself reports "*More* than half the inflow of development finance is now being offset by the return flow in the form of amortization, paying back of the loans, and interest. The annual debt service payments are becoming larger and larger proportions of the foreign exchange earnings of some of the developing countries. . . ." And with steadily diminishing foreign exchange earnings, needed to cover past loans, the capacity of these countries to earn further foreign exchange, and therefore to take care of their own private industrial needs, diminishes. Unless there are drastic changes, the time is very close at hand, a Bank senior officer has just reported, when the borrowers from some important underdeveloped countries "would have to pay back more each year than they actually receive" and accordingly, economic development — the very purpose of the lending operation itself — would come to a "grinding halt."*

---

*"The External Debt of the Developing Countries," address of Mr. S. Alde-

Mr. Woods has been alert to the self-defeating limitations of this long-prevailing approach to development financing. A new course has been charted. While the "bankable projects" and "economic justification" are not abandoned, what are called "soft loans" are proposed, where a bankable loan is unrealistic. Through what is called the International Development Association — the IDA — a World Bank affiliate, some countries may secure a fifty-year credit at little or no interest, repayable in soft rather than hard currency. This is not the conventional banker's loan at all, but one more nearly resembling a grant, preserving the form of indebtedness. But funds to make such "soft loans" or grants must come not from the private capital markets but from the taxpayers of donor countries rather than from the private capital markets.

For some time the principal hope for international development as expressed in the official circles is for a vastly greater inflow of money from the rich to the poorer countries. The rhetoric of officials and of intellectuals directed to this goal has been eloquent but quite unpersuasive as measured by results. Actually, thus far such an inflow of capital, far from greatly increasing is actually declining as a proportion of the income of the richer countries.

It is not going to be easy to persuade the richer countries — chiefly the U.S.A. and the European countries — to contribute large sums, running to billions, which IDA can then extend in the form of these fifty-year so-called loans. But it is a goal that deserves the most careful examination and thought of American leaders in private life as well as public. And time is running out. We are told officially at the recent meeting of the World Bank that "IDA's ability to undertake new commitments will terminate well before the end of the fiscal year"; that's a matter of months.

No single issue before the American Congress in the 1967 session, and in terms of world peace no single issue before the political and industrial leadership of this and other countries, exceeds in importance the question of enlarging the resources

wereld, to the Political Economy Association of the University of Uppsala, May 4, 1966.

fifty-one

of the International Development Association or of finding other means of meeting this urgent need. The prudent banker concept is breaking down fast. But when people are prepared to face up to their past miscalculations, this is a source of hope and redirection. And this is what is going on.

The rising tide of realism and candor is not confined to the failure of the "prudent banker concept." The development and managerial methods are getting a rousing self-examination, amounting at times to a rather rough going-over. I quote for example from a candid speech by the Associate Director of the Development Services Department of the World Bank, Mr. Michael L. Hoffman, an economist:*

"It is possible to dream of an [econometric] model" for a developing country — but the "model remains a dream . . . because almost none of the fundamental conditions for its functioning are present. . . .

". . . the obstacles to the rational handling of development finance are not primarily intellectual difficulties about how the process ought to work . . . the obstacles rise rather from *deep political and constitutional incompatibilities. . . .*" (My italics)

Now let me translate that phrase: "political and constitutional incompatibilities." These are nothing else than human problems, for political problems are human problems. The capacity to understand and to meet human problems is the core of the concept of the manager I have been describing, and I believe is the next long step in getting things done in the underdeveloped areas.

It has often been argued that systems analysis methods and computer programming techniques, so highly successful, brilliantly successful, in the design, let's say, of aircraft or missiles, can also solve the problems of the economic and social development of a country such as Greece or Algeria or Turkey or Nigeria. But because technicians use systems analysis to design rockets and missiles does not in itself qualify them to design human institutions and human motivations that are an inherent

---

*"Aid Coordination," presented to Ditchley Conference on Improving the Effectiveness of Aid for Overseas Development, June 3, 1966.

part, an integral part, of economic development. Men are not guided missiles; to guide human beings takes not systems analysis, but human understanding, and a sense of history. Gradually some of our technical brethren are coming to realize, I hope, that economic and political development is not just an exercise in systems analysis or econometrics; that what makes a mathematical model of development a "dream," may be the technician's lack of experience with the realities of human institutions and emotions. A sensitivity to and experience with human emotions, with history and with political institutions is, so far as I know, the only way this "incompatibility" between technique and reality can, in the long run, be overcome.

The American public and Congress thought we were being practical about "those foreigners," by bearing down on the terms of loans, being the stern banker and winning acclaim for our toughness. It hasn't turned out quite that way. Now the euphoria or hope in the phrase Decade of Development, and the moving rhetoric of the declarations at Punta del Este concerning Latin America are giving way not to despair or defeatism but realism, and a willingness to learn from experience. Here is the real hope.

That economic development overseas should come to a "grinding halt" for the great mass of humankind living in the poorer non-industrial countries would precipitate a series of disasters, compared to which the current agonies in Southeast Asia would be simply a curtain raiser. A disaster for these billions of people. A disaster for the prospects of the industrialized and the more affluent countries. No one has a complete answer to this crisis. But I dare to suggest that in the ideas and the energies of the President and top leadership of the international agency known as the World Bank and its affiliates lies the world's best present hope.

The leaders of American industry in this city, exemplified by the late Benjamin Fairless and by his present counterparts in industry, have always had great influence upon the thinking and action of American industry. Carnegie Institute of Technology, as much as any other educational center in America, has been a leader in the application of industrial thinking to critical public and human affairs. That you give this issue and these men in official life who confront it day by day the continuing benefit of your experience and judgment and influence is, I think, indeed a great contribution of industry to the peace of the world.

With a voice almost alone, and a sense of dedication unmatched in the officialdom of the entire Western world, the World Bank is working hard to secure a greater inflow of capital for the poorer countries. But the World Bank has also called for redoubled efforts to make development more effective; to make the money that is provided more effectively utilized. Money alone certainly won't suffice. Development is no one-way street. The less developed countries also need to accept greater and greater responsibility. The balance of my remarks tonight bear upon this necessity to make development methods within the underdeveloped countries more effective.

There is no single key to more effective development; there are many.

One vital component in making development efforts succeed is the practical application of the humanist concept of the managerial life. The decisive measure of the effectiveness of development assistance tendered from outside these countries is whether as a consequence of such assistance such a country's own development leadership is increased and strengthened — in the villages, in private industry, in governmental decision-making, and in administration.

The driving force of development, as I've observed, is the aroused energies and imagination and motivation of the people in the countries or regions where the development takes place. If development is to take place, it will be carried out, or not carried out, by these people. This is as true of the regions of America as it is true of Latin America or Asia or Africa. How effectively resources are used, and for what purpose, depends upon discovering, encouraging, and inspiring human talents, at all levels.

Parenthetically, this comment seems in order: If in the almost twenty years of aid to the underdeveloped countries the agencies involved have in fact given top priority to an increase in indigenous leadership and judgment about such a country's best interests, then it is fair to ask this question: Why is it that so many of these countries are still being treated as if they had learned very little in these years of tutelage and guidance? Surely this isn't true. If it isn't true, then why do the technical staffs of aiding agencies, national and multinational, and out-side experts, so often continue to conduct exhaustive and re-petitive reviews and to pass judgments on these countries with the very same particularity exercised a decade before? A school in which pupils never seem to be eligible for promotion to a higher grade would not seem to be a very good school.

On this matter of the better utilization of unrealized human potentialities, I shall try to sum up the results of my own experience in remote parts of the world; this is confirmed by years of experience in a once underdeveloped region of the United States, the Tennessee Valley.

Let me put it this way:

First: The less developed countries have underestimated — the leaders, the official leaders have underestimated — the potentialities of their own human energies and skills that should and can be devoted to those regions' development.

Second: As a corollary to this first proposition: we of the technically more developed nations have overestimated the importance to development progress of our own unquestioned ability to do *technical* tasks.

The consequences have been to inhibit the growth and ma-turing of indigenous talents; by our insensitivity to the way things look to the other fellow with a wholly different back-ground and culture, we have erected barriers between techni-cal people from the outside and the people in these countries who live there, who in the final analysis must do the develop-ing of their own country, if it is to be done at all.

These convictions about the great reservoir of unused human talents for leadership at all levels I had first tested in my experi-ence in the Tennessee Valley years ago, which at that time was an underdeveloped region of the United States. And they were not found wanting, in the Valley, judged by results in getting things done which required local business and civic leadership and participation, and the discovery and encouragement of latent abilities.

Is what we learned was true in an underdeveloped region of America also true in the less developed countries in distant parts of the world? I wanted to find out by the test of experience. Accordingly, some eleven years ago, I proposed the founding of a private development company operating on a business basis, that is to say for a profit or loss, dependent upon its own revenues and capital, but a corporation with public objectives. That enterprise has had more than a decade of trial, under difficult conditions, in Asia, in West Africa, and in Latin America. I shall refer to a few of the results.

In early 1956, somewhat over ten years ago, the Shah of Persia invited me to visit the eastern Mesopotamian plains of Iran — or Persia — there known as Khuzestan. Khuzestan had been a center of oil production, but little else. We were asked about the feasibility of restoring what had become a largely barren, bleak, disease-ridden and despairing desert area to the productivity and the strength which that same region enjoyed as the breadbasket and administrative center of the vast Persian world empire of ancient times. Our firsthand look persuaded us that this region, then so woebegone, did have the potentials for a rebuilding into a vigorous and highly productive area. We were directed to help translate this conviction into reality; accordingly our company was set to work on a huge program, largely using Iran's own funds.

After ten years the transformation is plain to be seen. Increases in the farmers' yields per hectare are very great. The villages and the villagers' lives, their health and morale have changed. Public health technology was an essential part of this process of change. The physical works that we planned, designed and had built — including one of the highest dams in the world — bring mountain-fed waters to the land. The electricity generated by this huge new Pahlavi dam adds its part in the transformation, making industry possible and rural life better.

But in the minds of all of us concerned in a managerial sense with helping Iran bring about these changes, we found that the most difficult barriers to development concerned not dams and canals and fertilizers; it concerned human beings. Human talents and leadership and human institutions must be found, or arise, in order that these physical activities would have any lasting meaning whatever. The great challenge to be overcome in the Khuzestan and upon which all else — the physical works, the engineering and agricultural technology — depended, was to stimulate and encourage and recognize latent Iranian talent. That capability would have to be found and encouraged within the hundreds of primitive villages in this region.

At the other end of the scale, there would have to be evidences of leadership among that minority, particularly the younger Persians who had the benefit of education. Moreover, the leadership would have to be translated into an organization that would fit the conditions of Iranian life and Iranian traditions. A spirit of hope and ferment and eagerness for change would have to grow in what at first seemed, I must say, most unlikely soil, if these physical changes were to bear fruit.

These qualities of leadership did not appear spontaneously, overnight. There were not a few setbacks, and some of them quite recent, and these still recur. I would be misstating the case if I said that during this ten-year period there have not been moments when one almost despaired. But the foundation upon which this transformation rests has been an unshakable faith in the great potentialities of virtually every human being in that region, those who were dispirited, lacking in hope, illiterate, afflicted with diseases of malnutrition, encumbered by an almost feudal state of land tenure, with few skills, with few roads, with the crudest of housing, with a precarious diet, with no schools or amenities, and most serious of all, a lack of encouragement or recognition of latent talents of leadership and management. And yet to a remarkable degree this first impression of the impossible human barriers has steadily been overcome.

Not so many years ago we used to refer to countries that were not as far along as we were as "backward" countries. Then we became more tactful and we referred to them as "underdeveloped" countries. And then we got even more tactful still, and now we refer to them as "developing" countries. But who is "backward" and who is "behind" is sometimes an open question. I ran into an episode that illustrates this, years ago. During World War II TVA was asked by the Lend-Lease Administration to design some dams behind the Urals for the Soviet Union, then our allies in the war. We were glad to do this as a part of the war effort. We had a large design staff and we set them to work. A group of Russians came to Knoxville, holed up in a hotel room and the work went on and they would look in on it now and then. One day the head of the Russian delegation called on our chief design engineer, Mr. Rich. Mr. Rich said, "I'm glad to see you. Have a seat." "No, I will not have a seat. Mr. Rich, I have come to complain." "What have you to complain about?" "I have come to complain. You are behind." "What do you mean, behind?" The Russian said, "The protocol between the Lend-Lease Administration and the U.S.S.R. provides that these dam designs shall be ready for us by the first of October. It is now the fifteenth of October and they are not ready. You are behind." Mr. Rich was a bit annoyed and said, "Now just a minute, just a minute. The protocol also said that you would have the basic data for us by the middle of June. It wasn't until early September that we had it. So *you* are behind." The Russian rared up and said, "Mr. Rich, I did not come here to complain about *my behind*; I came to complain about *your behind*." It's a little hard sometimes to know, especially after Sputnik, who's behind who. My own experience has been that there's a great deal more forwardness in some "backward" countries than we give them credit for.

In any case, what we Americans of my company found (perhaps we found it because we were looking for it in Persia) and what our Iranian colleagues found was that there were indeed able young Iranians who had potential leadership qualities. And many of the peasants, as they themselves call them — we would call them farmers or cultivators — though weakened by illness and with so little to hope for, before long became good farmers, perhaps the most complex of all tasks.

Beneath their superficial apathy was a strong impulse among these cultivators, these peasants, to improve their lives and give their children an education and a better chance. And among the very first utilizations of their surplus income in these villages is the building of schools. And one of the first things they do after the school is built of adobe is to put in some plate glass. As I said to some of my friends in an important glassworks here in this country, the idea of letting light into a school room became an important thing for these people to do. They wanted to give their children a better chance and a better opportunity, and in this they were at one with a great many other people in this country and elsewhere. In each of the scores of villages there were men with the ability to demonstrate to their fellows how things could be changed, whether dealing with sanitation, or raising and selling crops, or local roads or diet. The capacity of leadership to stimulate and to teach and to generate other leaders was there, awaiting only a chance to prove itself.

From the broader point of view of developing indigenous managerial leadership, however, perhaps the most far-reaching development was the creation by the Legislature of a Persian managerial instrumentality, the Khuzestan Water and Power Authority. This body was given responsibility for action, and for weaving together the various strands that make the physical and the non-physical or human factors in this transformation move ahead vigorously. But the creation of this body alone would have been without much meaning if there had not been Iranian leadership to man it, ready to undertake a new and pioneering venture of historic importance in a land of history. The Managing Director selected by the Shah was a young man, Abdol Reza Ansari,* whose deputies were Hassan Shahmirzadi and Ahmad Ali Ahmadi. These and other young Iranians in the Cabinet and in executive posts have been the decisive factor in the continued advance of the Khuzestan region.

We Americans at the outset were asked to provide and did provide complete managerial and technical services and experi-

---

*Recently made Minister of the Interior, succeeded by another young Iranian, Iradj Vahidi.

ence. Equally important, we had and expressed a point of view, a conviction, about the potentialities of development of the Khuzestan. The area is very hot. In the summer our people working on the dam were working in canyons at 130° Fahrenheit. But this climate is also an advantage in that one can have year-round cropping. To induce Iranians to come to this hot region was in itself quite a chore. But we quickly found that our efforts would have been futile entirely had it not been for those Iranians and the men they selected, who after this initial period took on increasing responsibilities in this enterprise. Today, Iranians are in full managerial control with us serving merely as advisors on the periphery; sometimes not so peripheral. And though our company continues to have a field force to assist in many ways, basically this is now — and will continue to be — an Iranian operation.

One's faith that leadership does exist at almost every level of life and training, from the most primitive village to the sophisticated and complex problems of planning and operating a huge enterprise has been amply justified. Disappointments and setbacks, some of them most disquieting, there certainly have been and I assume will always continue to be in Iran as everywhere in human affairs. But in the entire decade of experience in Southwest Persia, as an American who has spent most of his adult life in management, one thing stands out in my mind. It is that leadership will emerge and managerial talent will develop if the heart of the job to be done is conceived of as essentially one of stimulation, e.g., encouraging, inspiring, and bringing out those latent capacities of men which are the best hope of mankind and whose development are the center and focus of the managerial art, as they are, indeed, of democracy itself.

I could cite statistics about the remarkable increases in productivity and standards of living in that far-away region. But what impresses me the most, however, is not gross statistics. The most heartening thing is the rise of individual initiative among the people in the villages and farms of this once despairing region. There is among them a rising sense of enterprise in running their own affairs. These villagers have begun to develop a sense of community organization on their own. They have begun to demonstrate that they are learning the basic elements of business, by the way they make judgments about what to raise, when to sell and where, what is the right price, the use of credit, and so on and on; how to judge the fairness of charges for irrigation water, or how to use fertilizer to get a return from its use for themselves and their families. And the young men of Iran have shown a quick aptitude for industrial tasks too. It was only eighteen months after the completion of the Pahlavi Dam, a very complex operation indeed, until the operations themselves were in the hands of young Iranians with high school education and only a short period of training, and with no prior experience whatever in an industrial life. Experience has shown that Persians are far abler people in handling their own affairs than they had been given credit for, and than they had *given themselves* credit for.

The successful economic development in the upper Cauca Valley in southwest Colombia provides still another example that supports the theses I have been propounding. Twelve years ago we began working with and for a group of young business and professional men living in Cali, chief city of the Cauca Valley. Upon their initiative an autonomous public body was formed, the Cauca Valley Corporation — called CVC popularly — with these Colombian private citizens as its principal directors. The unusually rapid growth and development of that region, the fastest in all South America, industrially and agriculturally, is well known throughout Latin America; and people come from all parts of Latin America to observe the development of the Cauca Valley.

Here again I do not find the physical changes nor the statistics of economic growth — encouraging as they are — the most significant. More significant in terms of the still mysterious dynamics of the development process was the existence and performance of indigenous talents in that region. And that leadership was by no means confined to the physical and economic tasks of increasing power supply, the growth of industry, reclaiming and developing of lands, increasing food production, and so on.

sixty-one

It is the seemingly collateral and indirect stimulus of this leadership that has proved to be as important as the direct physical and economic consequences. What was generally thought to be a relatively backward and provincial area, the Cauca Valley, in a few years brought into being a distinguished regional university which continues to flourish and grow. I am told on the best of American medical authority that the Medical School and Hospital of this Universidad del Valle, in Cali, is probably the best in Latin America. Why did this happen? Because, I think, indigenous home-grown leadership was encouraged and recognized. And the brilliant young men who went to medical school in New York and elsewhere in this country, went back to Cali because they were encouraged to feel that here was a place for them, instead of staying away, as so many foreign students do after training in this country, feeling that there's no place for them at home, that they're not needed and recognized in their own country.

But there are other tangible consequences of a faith in people's capacity and they continue to multiply in the Cauca Valley. For example, on a recent visit to our work in Colombia one of the original directors of the Cauca Valley Corporation told me of the establishment of a philanthropic, private foundation, so far as I know the first one in South America, to provide education and health facilities for the thousands of impoverished country people who have poured into Cali from the surrounding hills. This foundation's work is financed by revenues from a gift of shares in the very successful private business of which this director of the CVC and his brothers are the owners.

When we cease to perpetuate the notion that only in the United States are there leaders of this public spirited frame of mind, and reject the popular American picture of the rich Latin Americans as irresponsible playboys, we will find, as many of us in private business have, that there are great reservoirs of initiative, public spirit, business sense, and humanist managerial leadership in most of the Latin American regions, and other parts of the world.

Certainly I have observed this in Venezuela, but also among

the young leaders of present Ghana, among the younger group of the citizens of the Ivory Coast in West Africa, and elsewhere. But the thesis that there is everywhere an untapped spring of local leadership to be recognized, encouraged, and given a chance is best illustrated, so far as my own experience is concerned, by my fourteen years here in America, in the Tennessee Valley.

When I first visited the town of Decatur in northern Alabama, now a flourishing industrial city, this town was in a state of economic and emotional despair. Its chief industry, a railroad shop, had left the town; things looked black. The most serious thing I found was a lack of self-confidence in the community's own leadership. When that returned (and how it returned is an interesting story), the town had turned the corner. One of the community's leaders of that dark time put the change that took place in words that epitomize the importance of human factors about which these lectures have been chiefly concerned. Mr. Barrett Shelton, publisher of a newspaper in Decatur, said:

"We can write of the great dams . . . of the building of home-grown industry and of electricity at last coming to the farms of thousands of farm people in this Valley. Yet the significant advance *has been in the thinking of a people.* . . . They can stand now and talk out in meeting. . . ."

The unexplained surges of human energies that have marked some periods of history had behind them some kind of central theme, some mystique that aroused people's spirits, their stamina, their imagination and ability to get things done. Economic development in the underdeveloped countries has yet to develop such a mystique. That it may come is one of the great hopes of our time. The evidence to support this hope and this faith is not entirely lacking.

If development adequate to meet the crisis of the widening gap between the rich and poor countries is to take place, it will take more than the infusion of huge amounts of capital, more than sophisticated techniques and mechanisms. It will require a grand mystique *from within* these underdeveloped countries. A great period of development will certainly not come from anything we have yet seen during the past twenty years of our efforts. That inspiration of men's spirits will not come merely by scolding the underdeveloped countries, nor their scolding us, nor from a we-know-better-than-thou attitude by foreign technical or financial experts. The soil for such a mystique of confidence that will nourish and give life to human capabilities will be the ability of these people to evolve ideas that suit their condition, and a greater recognition by them, as well as by us, of their latent capacity for leadership. Not that their own managers will not make mistakes aplenty. But Big Brother has made and is making his own share of mistakes. Like the rest of us, the people in the developing countries will learn from their own mistakes. But it may surprise and it may delight us how many successes they will make.

I close these lectures on the humanist concept of management by repeating the words of Montaigne I quoted in my opening lecture, who said that there are those "whose purpose it is to tell us what has happened. Mine, if I could attain it, would be to talk about what could happen." And to these words I would like to add my own: what I believe can be made to happen.   November 8, 1966

The following are questions put to Mr. Lilienthal by members of the audience, and his answers.

Q.   1) Don't you think that the formation of local cooperatives brings out managerial talents more quickly than other forms of enterprise? 2) The opportunity to attract and develop management talent probably varies between profit-oriented and non profit-oriented organizations. Which is superior?

A.   As to the first question I think one can't answer this categorically. We've had a series of unsuccessful managerial experiences with producers' cooperatives in this country. On the other hand, I think there's a great deal of experience to show that some cooperatives — such as in the rural electricity field — have created managerial leadership. One of the drawbacks is that though there's a small managerial group of very able people, the full membership of the cooperative soon falls

away and loses interest, and one no longer has a true cooperative enterprise. It's recently been necessary to have style shows
and I don't know what other kinds of entertainment to get the
members to come to even one annual meeting.

As to the second question about profit-oriented or non profit-oriented; I think there, too, I would not be able to be
categorical as to which is superior. My observation overseas has
been that the motive of private profit among people who are
relatively impoverished, people who have to push their way up
to get into the market economy, where they have to fight hard
to get more than enough to feed themselves—the profit incen-
tive has proved to be a very good way indeed of developing a
kind of leadership. So I have to give a kind of yes and no
answer to both questions.

Q. Can there be any real hope of progress in the near
future in those countries whose century-old traditions stand
directly in the way of real economic development? I refer
particularly to the recent riot in India protesting the slaughter
of sacred cows.

A. Clearly India, in my view, is the clinical case to end
clinical cases of difficulties of development. But a visit there
not very long ago has persuaded me that there is hope in spite
of many of the things that stand in the way, the cattle and the
monkeys and so on, religious feeling, a sense of violence.
Though the odds are very much against India, yet there are
affirmative components in India too, especially among the
younger generation. I think part of our own difficulty in judging
India's prospects is failure to recognize how strong is the un-
dercurrent among a generation just coming along who are
pretty well fed up to the teeth with the state of affairs in parts
of India.

On the affirmative side, religious sensibilities in India do not
stand in the way of some of the problems that Latin America
has, for example, in relation to the control of population. There
are no religious taboos against control of population in India.
The difficulties are administrative and lethargy and inadequate
education and motivation.

Q.   There are two questions here that fit together:
1. How would you propose to stimulate the flow of capital from the wealthy to the poor countries, when the wealthy countries are more concerned about the flow of wealth among themselves, that is, the balance of payment problem.
2. The second question suggests, perhaps, that soft payments, soft loans and return in soft currency may not be quite as difficult, and perhaps this is the solution to the problem.
A.   How to get the affluent countries, including the United States, to contribute to the building up of other countries, through the World Bank or otherwise, is something we've been struggling with for a long time. We thought we had it pretty well solved by the device of loans, carefully selected, carefully examined. This turned out not to be a solution; quite the contrary for the countries who need it the most. Looking at the picture outside our country we find West Germany or England confronted with problems of needing capital themselves. And in our own country we have just over the horizon almost every other month a new kind of problem for us, a balance of payments problem, an outflow of gold. How under these circumstances George Woods is going to crack this one I leave to his superior wisdom and persuasive powers. But I think European countries — as well as ourselves — must come to see this is broadly in their interest, not because they sell goods in these countries, but broadly in our interest and in the interests of peace in the same sense that we would not hesitate to spend money, and large amounts to protect our friends overseas in a military sense.
I would have great difficulty in finding any other reason than simply that it's the American thing to do, so far as the American public is concerned. I doubt if that argument has much appeal to European nations who are now well-to-do to increase their proportion of contribution which is still very small. If the contributions from Europe were to be doubled, I think the American public would find a way and find it much more persuasive to make larger contributions lest development overseas come to a grinding halt and lest famine and revolution in the next ten years beset the world.

Q. People are concerned about the problem of indigenous leadership and how one develops it and several people have wondered to what extent formally are our Peace Corps and people who give courses and institutes overseas being encouraged to look for that leadership and to report it.

A. This varies a good deal, but by and large I think among aid and lending missions abroad there's a tendency to downgrade indigenous leadership.

We send overseas a good many people who are highly skilled in a certain kind of cattle breeding, say. They find it difficult to believe that anyone who hasn't spent his whole life raising Holsteins and breeding them can know very much about cattle. Well, Holsteins may have nothing to do with that country; that may not be their kind of cattle; and any kind of cattle may not be a central problem at all. So there is a kind of looking-down-the-nose contempt for local talent. This is part of the problem. My own limited experience with the Peace Corps has been quite otherwise. But these are youngsters. They're cock-sure about their energies and their desire to learn about the world, but fortunately they don't come touted as experts. I think too often the technical and managerial people who've gone abroad have tended to overlook indigenous talents because superficially they don't look like the kind of fellows they were in college with. This is a serious mistake.

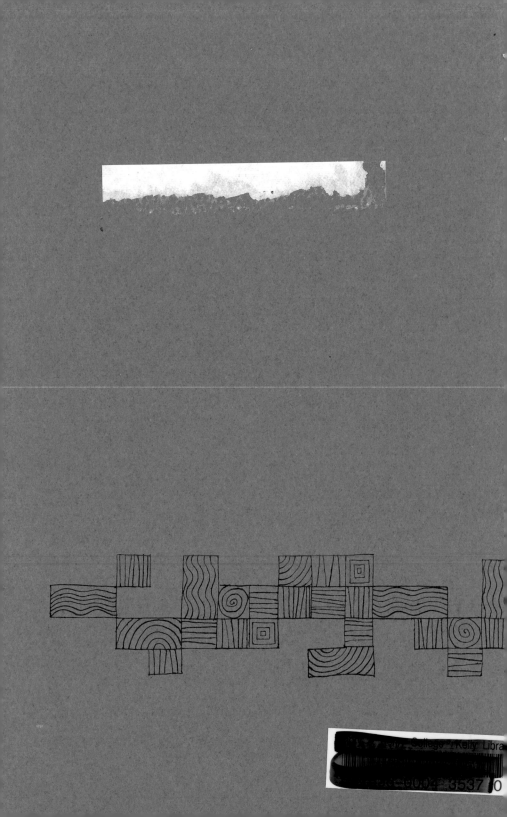